# The Jesus Story

For Christmas and Easter and Every Day In Between

By Kathy Hardee

Copyright 2020 by Kathy Hardee

All Scripture quotations are from the ESV Bible (The Holy Bible, English Standard Version), copyright 2001 by Crossway Bibles, a publishing ministry of Good News Publishers. Used by permission. All rights reserved.

For my grandchildren: Tyler, Luke, Kendall, Ashlyn, Brantley, Kalena and Leah. May you know the love of God through Jesus Christ our Savior and Lord.

Now to him who is able
to keep you from stumbling
and to present you blameless
before the presence of his glory
with great joy,
to the only God, our Savior,
through Jesus Christ our Lord,
be glory, majesty, dominion,
and authority, before all time
and now and forever. Amen.
Jude 24-25

# Introduction

*The Jesus Story* introduces Jesus as the Messiah God promised many years ago. That truth is expanded to include Jesus' birth, sinless life, deity, death, burial and resurrection. The story is divided into twelve sections. It can be told all at once, or over a period of days leading up to Christmas or Easter.

At the back of the book is a list of objects that can be purchased and put into twelve gift boxes or plastic eggs. First read the story and the Bible verse. Then open the corresponding egg or gift box, and talk about it. The objects are meant to spark imagination and meaningful conversation. There's a shopping list on the last page that you can tear out and bring with you to the store.

If you tell the story at Easter, put the objects in numbered eggs. Use gift boxes or bags, if you tell the story at Christmas. To encourage interest and excitement, put a few new items in the containers each time you tell the story, and let the children keep the items.

Additional Scripture references are noted for use in the classroom or with older children.

*The Jesus Story* is a fun way to share the gospel. It's meant to be told over and over again, year after year.

## Day One

A long time ago, God came to earth. God actually became a baby! An angel told His mother, Mary, to name Him Jesus. We celebrate His birthday every Christmas.

And the angel said to her,
***"Do not be afraid, Mary, for you have found favor with God. And behold, you will conceive in your womb and bear a son, and you shall call His name Jesus"*** (Luke 1:30-31, also Matthew 1:23).

(open #1)

The angel told Mary she would have a baby boy. And she did!

## Day Two

Jesus grew up just like every other little boy grows up. But He didn't act like any other little boy. Jesus never lied. He never cheated. He never said an unkind word, or did an unkind thing. And Jesus never, not even once, disobeyed His parents. Jesus never sinned! He never did anything wrong.

The Bible says,
***"The child [Jesus] grew and became strong, filled with wisdom. And the favor of God was upon Him"*** (Luke 2:40).

(open #2)

Do you think Jesus played with marbles? Maybe He did. He might have played with blocks, too.

Have you ever said an unkind word, or disobeyed your parents? The Bible says everyone has sinned. Jesus is the only one who never sinned. (see Romans 3:23)

# Day Three

God told the people of Israel He would give them a King, their very own Messiah.  The Messiah would love them and forgive them and show them how to live. The people waited and waited for their King. It seemed He would never come. But they kept waiting and hoping and looking for their King. Then, one day, a man named Andrew met Jesus.

After Andrew met Jesus, he hurried to Simon, his brother, and said,
***"We have found the Messiah"*** (John 1:41).

(open #3)

Do you think Jesus wore a crown? No, He didn't. The first time Jesus came to earth, He came as God's servant. But when He comes to earth again, He will come as King of Kings and Lord of Lords. Then everyone will bow down to Him. (See Philippians 2:9-11)

# Day Four

Jesus performed miracles to prove that He and God are one. He healed many people who were sick. He told a storm to stop, and it did! He walked on water. He turned one little boy's lunch into enough food to feed over 5,000 hungry people. And He brought a dead person back to life. Only God could do those things!

Jesus said, ***"I and the Father are one"*** (John 10:30).

(open #4)

A long time ago, men wrote God's word on parchment paper, and rolled it into scrolls. Now the Bible is a book. We learn about God, and get to know Him, when we read the Bible. It's filled with true stories about Jesus! Do you like to hear true stories? (see John 20:30-31)

# Day Five


Jesus loved people more than anyone ever could. Some people loved and followed Jesus. Other people hated Him. They didn't want to obey Him, or bow down to Him as King. They wanted to kill Him.

The Bible says,
***"For God so loved the world, that He gave His only son, that whoever believes in Him should not perish but have eternal life"*** (John 3:16).

(open #5)

Did you know that God loves you?  He wants you to love Him, too. When we love God, we want to obey Him. (see 1 John 4:19, John 14:15)

## Day Six

On the night before Jesus died, He ate supper with His friends. He told them about His plan to go back to heaven, and prepare a place for them. He said one day they would live with Him in heaven.

Jesus said,
***"If I go and prepare a place for you, I will come again and will take you to myself, that where I am you may be also"*** (John 14:3).

(open #6)

What do you think heaven will be like? Do you think there will be houses?  The Bible says God will live with His people, and there will be no crying or sickness or pain. The streets will be made of gold! Everything will be made new. (see Revelation 21:3-4)

## Day Seven

After Jesus ate supper with His friends, He prayed for them. Jesus knew He would be killed. And He knew His friends would be very sad. So He asked His Father to take care of them.

Jesus lifted up His eyes to heaven and said, ***"They are in the world, and I am coming to You. Holy Father, keep them in your name"*** (John 17:11).

(open #7)

Prayer is talking to God the same way you talk to your mom or dad, or grandma or grandpa. God likes it when we talk to Him. (see Philippians 4:6-7)

What are some things you can pray about?

# Day Eight

When Jesus finished praying, a mob of angry men came and took Him away. They put Him on trial, and declared Him guilty, even though He had never done anything wrong. They decided to kill Him by hanging Him on a cross—but that didn't surprise Jesus at all. He wanted to take the punishment for our sin, and He knew He would die on a cross.

One day, Jesus said, ***"…the Son of Man [must] be lifted up, that whoever believes in Him may have eternal life"*** (John 3:14-15).

(open #8)

Jesus died on a cross to take the punishment for sin. Do you know what sin is?

Sin separates us from God, because God is Holy. Everything He does is good and right and true. He never lies, or does anything wrong.

We can tell God we're sorry for the things we've done wrong. We can ask Him to forgive us, and He will! Do you know why? Because Jesus took the punishment for everyone who believes in Him.

# Day Nine


While Jesus hung on the cross, people mocked Him. They said, "If you are God, save yourself!" And Jesus could have saved Himself. He could have called for ten thousand angels to rescue Him. But He didn't, because He wanted to take the punishment for the sins of God's people.

The people who watched Jesus on the cross wagged their heads and said,
***"If you are the Son of God, come down from the cross. He saved others; he cannot save himself. He trusts in God; let God deliver him now"*** (Matthew 27:40, 42-43).

(open #9)

Did you know that angels do whatever God tells them to do? Sometimes He sends them to protect His people. (see Matthew 26:53, Psalm 91:11-12)

## Day Ten

After Jesus died, two of His friends took Him off the cross. They wrapped His body in strips of cloth and sweet-smelling spices. Then they laid Him in a tomb.

The Bible says,
***"So they took the body of Jesus and bound it in linen cloths with the spices, as is the burial custom of the Jews"*** (John 19:40).

(open #10)

Jesus died, and His friends were very sad, but God has power over life and death. Something exciting happened three days after Jesus died! Do you think you know the end to this true story?

## Day Eleven

Strong men rolled a huge stone in front of Jesus' tomb, so no one could get in and no one could take Jesus out.

The Bible says they ***"rolled a great stone to the entrance of the tomb and went away"*** (Matthew 27:60).

(open #11)

A tomb was like a cave, with an opening at the front, so people could walk in and out. How big do you think the stone had to be to close the entrance of a tomb? Do you think it was bigger than you?

# Day Twelve

Three days after Jesus died, three of His friends went to the tomb. They were women who wanted to put more spices on Jesus' body. On the way to the tomb, they said to each other, "Who will roll away the stone for us?" When they got to the tomb, an angel had already rolled away the stone. When they went inside, they found an empty tomb!

The angel said to the women,
*"Do not be afraid, for I know that you seek Jesus who was crucified. He is not here, for He has risen, as He said…go quickly and tell His disciples that He has risen from the dead"* (Matthew 28:5-7).

After Jesus finished all the work God gave Him to do, God brought Him back to life. And He still lives, to this very day!

(open #12)

Why do you think there's soap in our last egg (or box)?

Thanks to Jesus, we can ask God to wash away our sins. And He will!

The Bible says:
***"If we confess our sins, He is faithful and just to forgive us our sins and to cleanse us from all unrighteousness"*** (1 John 1:9).

When we confess our sins, we agree with God that our sin deserves punishment.

After we confess our sins, we can be glad, because we know Jesus took the punishment for our sins.

Jesus came to His own people, but they didn't care about Him or love Him. They didn't want to obey Him or honor Him as King.

But all who believe Him and receive Him as Savior and Lord become children of God (see John 1:11-12).

You can pray to God right now and ask God to forgive your sins and become Your very own Lord and Savior. And then He will help you live a life that is fully pleasing to Him.

Let's pray!

Bible Verses Referenced in the Story

***"Do not be afraid, Mary, for you have found favor with God. And behold, you will conceive in your womb and bear a son, and you shall call His name Jesus"*** (Luke 1:30-31, also Matthew 1:23).

***"The child [Jesus] grew and became strong, filled with wisdom. And the favor of God was upon Him"*** (Luke 2:40).

***"We have found the Messiah"*** (John 1:41).

Jesus said, ***"I and the Father are one"*** (John 10:30).

***"For God so loved the world, that He gave His only son, that whoever believes in Him should not perish but have eternal life"*** (John 3:16).

***"They are in the world, and I am coming to You. Holy Father, keep them in your name"*** (John 17:11).

One day, Jesus said, ***"…the Son of Man [must] be lifted up, that whoever believes in Him may have eternal life"*** (John 3:14-15).

The people who watched Jesus on the cross wagged their heads and said,

*"If you are the Son of God, come down from the cross. He saved others; he cannot save himself. He trusts in God; let God deliver him now"* (Matthew 27:40, 42-43).

*"So they took the body of Jesus and bound it in linen cloths with the spices, as is the burial custom of the Jews"* (John 19:40).

The Bible says they *"rolled a great stone to the entrance of the tomb and went away"* (Matthew 27:60).

The angel said to the women,
*"Do not be afraid, for I know that you seek Jesus who was crucified. He is not here, for He has risen, as He said…go quickly and tell His disciples that He has risen from the dead"* (Matthew 28:5-7).

*"If we confess our sins, He is faithful and just to forgive us our sins and to cleanse us from all unrighteousness"* (1 John 1:9).

<u>Here's what you'll need:</u>

Twelve eggs or gift bags or boxes numbered 1-12.

<u>Egg/Box 1:</u> any small item found in the baby shower section of stores, an It's a Boy trinket, or small piece of baby blanket

<u>Egg/Box 2:</u> marbles, a small bouncy ball, small blocks or toy

<u>Egg/Box 3:</u> crown (charm or sticker)

<u>Egg/Box 4:</u> rolled up Scripture (copied from page of Bible), picture of Bible, Bible charm or sticker

<u>Egg/Box 5:</u> heart (plenty of options to choose from)

<u>Egg/Box 6:</u> Monopoly game house, pictures of houses from real estate section, a piece of candy wrapped in gold foil, gold wrapped chocolate coins

<u>Egg/Box 7:</u> praying hands (charm, clipart cutout, or sticker)

<u>Egg/Box 8:</u> cross (many options to choose from)

<u>Egg/Box 9</u>: angel or wings (charm or sticker)
If you get wings, say, "Did you know angels really do have wings? Some have six!" (see Isaiah 6:2)

<u>Egg/Box 10</u>: strips of muslin/cloth, spices such as cloves, all spice berries, nutmeg

<u>Egg/Box 11</u>: stone

<u>Egg/Box 12</u>: soap (small soap ball or bath bomb, piece of a bar of soap)

(There's a shopping list on the last page for you to tear out and bring with you to the store.)

Dear Friend in the Lord,

I hope you enjoyed sharing the gospel! Please let me know how it went and how I can pray for you. You can email me at kathy@kathyhardee.com. I always respond to emails, so if you don't hear back from me, I may not have received your email. You can find me @kathyhardee on Instagram, or visit my blog, *One Minute with God*, at www.kathyhardee.com/blog.

Turn this little book into a keepsake by using the last blank pages to share your Christmas and Easter memories, have your children draw a picture, or write a prayer. Don't forget to include the date for future reference.

God's best to you!
Kathy

# My Favorite Christmas Memories

# My Favorite Easter Memories

The Day I Asked Jesus to be My Savior

Dear Jesus, I love you because…

Our Christmas Tree

# My Family

<u>Shopping List</u>

Twelve eggs or gift bags or boxes. Number them 1-12.

Egg/Box 1: any small item found in the baby shower section of stores, an It's a Boy trinket, or small piece of baby blanket

Egg/Box 2: marbles, a small bouncy ball, small blocks or toy

Egg/Box 3: crown (charm or sticker)

Egg/Box 4: rolled up Scripture (copied from page of Bible), picture of Bible, Bible charm or sticker

Egg/Box 5: heart (plenty of options to choose from)

Egg/Box 6: Monopoly game house, pictures of houses from real estate section, a piece of candy wrapped in gold foil, gold wrapped chocolate coins

Egg/Box 7: praying hands (charm, clipart cutout, or sticker)

Egg/Box 8: cross (many options to choose from)

Egg/Box 9: angel or wings (charm or sticker)

Egg/Box 10: strips of muslin/cloth, spices such as cloves, allspice berries, or nutmeg

Egg/Box 11: stone

Egg/Box 12: soap (small soap ball or bath bomb, piece of a bar of soap)

9 798615 760365